DMITRI KABALEVSKY
THE GALLOPING COMEDIANS
(COMEDIANS' GALLOP)

ARRANGED FOR XYLOPHONE OR MARIMBA AND PIANO BY MORRIS GOLDENBERG

G. SCHIRMER, Inc.

DISTRIBUTED BY

HAL•LEONARD®
CORPORATION
7777 W. BLUEMOUND RD. P.O. BOX 13819 MILWAUKEE, WI 53213

THE GALLOPING COMEDIANS
(COMEDIANS' GALLOP)

Dmitri Kabalevsky
Arranged for Xylophone or Marimba and Piano by
Morris Goldenberg

4

THE GALLOPING COMEDIANS
(COMEDIANS' GALLOP)

Xylophone or Marimba Solo

Dmitri Kabalevsky
Arranged for Xylophone or Marimba and Piano by
Morris Goldenberg

Presto (♩ = 200)

DMITRI KABALEVSKY · THE GALLOPING COMEDIANS (COMEDIANS' GALLOP)

XYLOPHONE OR MARIMBA AND PIANO

U.S. $8.99

ISBN 978-1-4234-7758-7

HL50490097